THERAPY DOGS
ON THE JOB

BY MARNE VENTURA

Published by The Child's World®
1980 Lookout Drive • Mankato, MN 56003-1705
800-599-READ • www.childsworld.com

Photographs ©: Doug Bauman/The Daily Oakland Press/AP Images,
cover, 1; Spc. Taryn Hagerman, 40th Public Affairs Detachment/US Army,
5; Shutterstock Images, 6, 12; Sgt. Keenan Zelazoski/US Marine Corps, 8;
Kristen Wong/US Marine Corps, 9; Amy J. Correnti/Rockford Register Star/
AP Images, 10; Jocelyn Augustino/FEMA, 13, 20; Monkey Business Images/
Shutterstock Images, 14; Aaron Cole/Aurora Sentinel/AP Images, 16; Airman
1st Class Zachary Wolf/US Air Force, 17; iStockphoto, 18

ISBN 9781503816183

LCCN 2016945653

Printed in the United States of America
PA02318

TABLE OF
CONTENTS

Fast Facts 4

Chapter 1
Kicker, the Therapy Dog 7

Chapter 2
Becoming a Therapy Dog 11

Chapter 3
Therapy for Kicker 19

Think About It 21
Glossary 22
To Learn More 23
Selected Bibliography 23
Index 24
About the Author 24

FAST FACTS

The Job

- Therapy dogs go with their **handlers** to schools, hospitals, and nursing homes.
- The dogs visit people with mental or physical illness.
- The dogs give people comfort, company, and attention.
- Some therapy dogs and handlers work as volunteers. For others, it is their full-time job.

Training Time

- Dogs must be at least one year old to become therapy dogs.
- Therapy dogs are trained to be well-behaved and calm around people.
- Dogs who qualify must pass a one-hour test and three test visits by an expert.

Common Breeds

- Many types of dogs can be therapy dogs.
- A therapy dog must have a calm **temperament**. It must stay relaxed in new environments.

Famous Dogs

- Lexy, a German shepherd, helped soldiers in the early 2000s recover after serving in a war.

- A pit bull named Elsa suffered a bad injury in 2010. After her injury, she needed to walk with a special cart. Elsa became a therapy dog for people who had trouble walking due to injury.

Chapter 1

KICKER, THE THERAPY DOG

Kicker walked into the nursing home. The golden retriever was only one year old. He stayed close to his handler, Jo Anne Fusco. The two had just finished training as a therapy dog team. It was their first visit. The people in this nursing home had memory loss and other illnesses. Kicker looked around the room. **Elderly** people were sitting around the room or walking about.

Kicker walked up to a woman seated close by. He settled his head into her lap. He gazed up into her eyes. He wagged his tail. The patient smiled and rested her hand on Kicker's blond fur. Her face relaxed. Kicker closed his eyes and waited.

◀ **Therapy dogs provide company to people who may have a hard time leaving their homes.**

Kicker stayed with the woman until she lifted her hand. Then he moved on to the next patient.

For ten years after that first day on the job, Kicker and Fusco visited **cancer** patients, special education students, hospitalized children, and the elderly.

▲ **Therapy dogs help cheer up people who are going through difficult times.**

▲ Some therapy dogs listen to kids as they read. The dogs can help the kids feel more confident reading aloud.

Kicker was a natural therapy dog. He was friendly and gentle. He seemed to sense when a person wanted him to get close. He gave comfort and joy to sick and sad people.

But one day, Kicker seemed tired. He was not eating. He had lost weight. Something was wrong with Kicker.

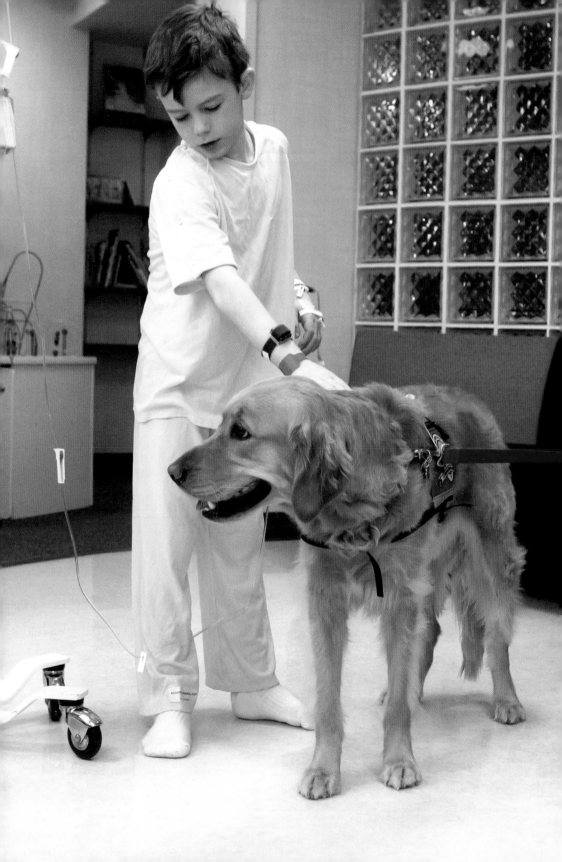

Chapter 2

BECOMING A THERAPY DOG

The first therapy dog did not have training like Kicker. She was a Yorkshire terrier named Smoky. Smoky walked into the hospital where her owner was staying after World War II. He had been hurt in the war. His friends thought Smoky might cheer him up. Smoky not only cheered up her owner, but other patients also smiled when they saw the dog. The nurses at the hospital asked if Smoky could stay. Since then, organizations have set up standards for therapy dogs. Therapy dogs and their owners must pass tests to become an official therapy dog team.

◀ Therapy dogs work in hospitals to distract and cheer up patients going through treatment.

▲ **Many breeds of dogs can become therapy dogs.**

Golden retrievers, pit bulls, corgis, and German shepherds line up with their owners. They are at an organization that tests therapy dog teams. All of the dogs are at least one year old, but some are older. The dogs sit and stay calmly next to their owners. Each dog has had **obedience** training and gotten its **vaccinations**. The dogs are well-groomed and clean.

In the first test, the testers watch how the dogs take commands. Some of the dogs sniff and paw at other dogs too much. Others bark or whine. These dogs need more training before they can become therapy dogs.

▲ **Therapy dogs must be able to stay calm around strangers.**

Next the testers try to distract and unsettle the dogs. The testers walk on crutches near the dogs. They make startling noises. They open up umbrellas. One of the dogs gets nervous when the tester opens an umbrella. The dog backs away from his handler. This dog will also need to take the test again before becoming a therapy dog.

The testers also check to see how the dogs react to strangers. They touch the dogs on the face and body. They hold the dogs' tails and paws. They pull on the dogs' collars and hug the dogs.

A handful of the dogs pass all the tests. They get vests or bandannas with badges on them. That way people know the dog is doing a special job.

Therapy dogs must get used to the environment they will be in. Kayla, a brown boxer with three legs, works in a nursing home. She got used to being around medical equipment, wheelchairs, and motorized scooters.

◀ **Therapy dogs must be comfortable being held and hugged.**

▲ **Therapy dogs can help distract patients from painful physical therapy.**

Children such as three-year-old Naomi or 12-year-old Sam have illnesses that make it hard for them to move their arms or legs. They have to go to physical therapy. Prairie, a golden retriever therapy dog, makes it fun for Naomi and Sam. The dog distracts them from doing exercises that hurt. Having the dog nearby to pet or hold helps the children feel better.

Five-year-old toy poodle Nala comes to work every day with her owner. The man works at a home for seniors who cannot live on their own because of medical problems. Nala is a facility therapy dog. Every day she goes from room to room and spends time with each patient. It cheers and comforts them to pet her and to spend time with her.

▲ **Some therapy dogs visit patients at the same place every day.**

Chapter 3

THERAPY FOR KICKER

Kicker's handler Jo Anne Fusco took him to the **veterinarian** to find out what was wrong. The vet gave Fusco some bad news. Kicker had cancer. He had to stop making visits to sick people. He needed **chemotherapy**.

The vet gave Kicker medicine that made him better. After treatment, he was able to go back to work. When Kicker visited cancer patients, Fusco told them Kicker had been treated for cancer, too.

Seven-year-old Brian had cancer for three years. He spent most of his time in the hospital. Kicker started visiting Brian. Kicker stayed with him during chemotherapy. He rested his head in Brian's lap.

◄ Veterinarians help make sure therapy dogs are healthy.

▲ Therapy dogs often work with people in need, including those who have been through major disasters.

He even got up on the bed with Brian. Brian's wish, when he was done with the hospital, was to have a dog just like Kicker.

Kicker lived to be 14 years old. In his lifetime, he visited thousands of people. He cheered them up, kept them company, and made them smile. He won several awards and was in a Westminster Kennel Club competition in 2005. He was even a guest on the *Today* show a few times. There is an old saying that dogs are humans' best friends. Therapy dogs such as Kicker show this. They are selfless, loyal, loving friends to people in need.

THINK ABOUT IT

- Therapy dogs are often selected because they have an even temperament. Why does this matter?
- How might a therapy dog help a shy or frightened child relax?
- What kind of facts would support the claim that therapy dogs help people?

GLOSSARY

cancer (KAN-sur): Cancer is a disease caused by unusual cell division. Therapy dogs comfort cancer patients.

chemotherapy (kee-moh-THAIR-uh-pee): Chemotherapy is a treatment that kills cancer cells. Therapy dogs keep cancer patients company during chemotherapy.

elderly (EL-dur-lee): An old or aged person is elderly. Therapy dogs visit the elderly in nursing homes.

handlers (HAND-lurs): Handlers are people who train animals. Therapy dogs and their handlers work as a team to visit people in need.

obedience (oh-BEE-dee-ens): Obedience is the act of following directions. Therapy dogs must first pass basic obedience training.

temperament (TEM-pur-uh-muhnt): Temperament is an animal's nature and behavior. Therapy dogs need to have a calm, friendly temperament.

vaccinations (vak-suh-NAY-shuhns): Vaccinations are substances that prevent diseases. Therapy dogs must have vaccinations to keep them from getting sick.

veterinarian (vet-ur-uh-NAIR-ee-uhn): A veterinarian is a medical doctor for animals. Therapy dogs go to a veterinarian to make sure they are in good health.

TO LEARN MORE

Books

Gagne, Tammy. *Ways to Help Chronically Ill Children*. Hockessin, DE: Mitchell Lane, 2011.

Goldish, Meish. *R.E.A.D. Dogs*. New York: Bearport, 2015.

Green, Sara. *Therapy Dogs*. Minneapolis, MN: Bellwether Media, 2014.

Person, Stephen. *Great Dane: Gentle Giant*. New York: Bearport, 2012.

Web Sites

Visit our Web site for links about therapy dogs: childsworld.com/links

Note to Parents, Teachers, and Librarians: We routinely verify our Web links to make sure they are safe and active sites. So encourage your readers to check them out!

SELECTED BIBLIOGRAPHY

Swartz, Anna. "Poodle Goes Door to Door at Nursing Home. Every Day. All by Herself." *The Dodo*. The Dodo.com, 15 Apr. 2016. Web. 30 Jun. 2016.

"Therapy Dog Program." *AKC.org*. American Kennel Club, 2016. Web. 30 Jun. 2016.

"What Is a 'Therapy Dog'?" *Therapy Dogs of Vermont*. Therapy Dogs of Vermont, 2015. Web. 30 Jun. 2016.

Wolff, Cindy. "Therapy Dog Brought Calm, Comfort to Sufferers." *KnoxNews.com*. Knoxville News Sentinel, 2 Mar. 2015. Web. 30 Jun. 2016.

INDEX

boxer, 15

cancer, 8, 19
chemotherapy, 19
corgi, 12

elderly, 7–8
Elsa (dog), 5

Fusco, Jo Anne,
    7–8, 19

German shepherd,
    5, 12
golden retriever, 7,
    12, 16

Kayla (dog), 15
Kicker (dog), 7–9,
    11, 19–21

Lexy (dog), 5

Nala, 17
nursing home, 4,
    7, 15

obedience, 12

pit bull, 5, 12
Prairie (dog), 16

Smoky (dog), 11
soldier, 5

test, 4, 11–13, 15
toy poodle, 17

vaccination, 12
veterinarian, 19

Westminster
    Kennel Club,
    21

ABOUT THE AUTHOR

Marne Ventura is the author of 37 books for kids. She loves writing about nature, science, technology, health, food, and crafts. She is a former elementary school teacher, and she holds a master's degree in education. Marne lives with her husband on the central coast of California.